TO

FROM

D0602939

DATE

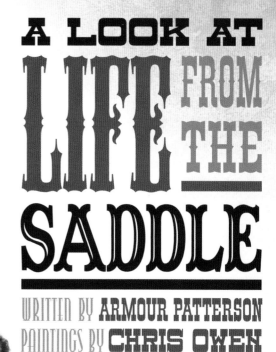

A LOOK AT
LIFE FROM THE
SADDLE

WRITTEN BY **ARMOUR PATTERSON**
PAINTINGS BY **CHRIS OWEN**

HARVEST HOUSE PUBLISHERS
EUGENE, OREGON

Design and production by Koechel Peterson & Associates, Inc., Minneapolis, Minnesota

Chris Owen is published by Somerset Fine Art. For more information about Mr. Owen and his work, please visit www.somersetfineart.com.
All artwork © Chris Owen

Bibliography: J. Frank Dobie, *Cow People* (New York: University of Texas, 1981); Richard W. Slatta, *Cowboys of the Americas* (New Haven: Yale University Press, 1990); Virginia Cowan-Smith and Bonnie Domrose Stone, *Aloha Cowboy* (Honolulu: University of Hawaii Press, 1988); and David Dary, *Cowboy Culture* (Lawrence, KS: University Press of Kansas, 1989).

A LOOK AT LIFE FROM THE SADDLE
Copyright © 2011 Text by Armour Patterson; Artwork by Chris Owen
Published by Harvest House Publishers
Eugene, Oregon 97402
www.harvesthousepublishers.com

ISBN 978-0-7369-2912-7

Printed in China

11 12 13 14 15 16 17 18 19 / **FC** / 10 9 8 7 6 5 4 3 2 1

> LIVE A GOOD,
> HONORABLE LIFE.
> THEN, WHEN YOU
> GET OLDER
> AND THINK BACK,
> YOU'LL ENJOY IT A
> SECOND TIME.
>
> COWBOY PROVERB

CONTENTS

GOD SAW ALL THAT HE HAD MADE,
AND IT WAS VERY GOOD.
THE BOOK OF GENESIS

LIFE IN THE SADDLE: THE COWBOY'S HEART

*Happiness is inward, and not outward; and so,
it does not depend on what we have, but on what we are.*

HENRY VAN DYKE

Due to the unfortunate realities of economics and politics, there are fewer ranchers and fewer cowboys with each passing year. Despite this march of so-called progress, the cowboys of the American West, Mexico, and Hawaii left a trail and legacy that cannot be buried or tarnished by time, technological advances, or revisionism. Like a red-hot branding iron touched to the soul, their imprint on the collective heart, mind, and psyche of those who followed is here for the duration.

Though few today will ever live a cowboy's life or do his work, all who so desire, regardless of location or occupation, can live the cowboy way. No "cowboy code" or "code of the West" was written down before the advent of Western genre films and television shows. Rather, "the code" was an unspoken sense of responsibilities and expectations for men of that time and place. Violators of that code and newcomers who didn't learn it quickly had no place among such men for long.

So cowboy up! The same virtues that made a good man or woman in 1870 will make good ones in the twenty-first century too. You can't change the world, but you can make it a better place. That happens when you make yourself a better person. No matter how you dress or what you do, here is the code you can cowboy up by.

THE COWBOY CODE

- Speak the truth and let your word be your bond.

- Never betray a trust or desert a friend.

- Protect and care for those who can't help themselves.

- Be gentle with women, children, and the elderly.

- Care for animals and protect the land.

- Be courteous, polite, and neat.

- Learn all you can and cultivate wisdom.

- Speak straight, speak properly, and don't speak too much.

- Do the job you're paid to do with pride and honor.

- Never quit when times are toughest.

- It's fine to feel fear, but don't let it back you down.

- Remember that good never prevails without courage and grit.

- If something sounds too good to be true, expect that it is.

- Keep your sense of humor and don't meddle.

- When you've done all you can, rest in your faith.

They were loyal to their outfit and to one another. A man that was not square could not long remain with an outfit...Every man would sacrifice his life to protect the herd.

GRANVILLE STUART, CATTLEMAN, MONTANA

Climb the mountains and get their good tidings. Nature's peace will flow into you as sunshine flows into trees. The winds will blow their own freshness into you, and the storms their energy, while cares will drop off like autumn leaves.

JOHN MUIR

You have made known to me the path of life; you will fill me with joy in your presence, with eternal pleasures at your right hand.

THE BOOK OF PSALMS

FAITHFULNESS SPRINGS FORTH FROM THE EARTH,
AND RIGHTEOUSNESS LOOKS DOWN FROM HEAVEN.
THE BOOK OF PSALMS

A COWBOY'S HONOR LEADS THE WAY

Men are born equal, free and are distinguished alone by virtue.

LORENZO DE ZAVALA, TEXAS PATRIOT AND
FIRST VICE PRESIDENT OF THE REPUBLIC OF TEXAS

Honor so imbued every facet of a cowboy's life and being that discussion of him apart from that virtue would be amiss. Honor influenced and determined how he lived, who he worked for, what work he would do, who he respected and did not respect, when he would or wouldn't fight, to which persons and principles he would be loyal, and how he treated women, children, the elderly, animals, and even strangers. Where there is no honor there is little virtue. All of cowboys' attributes and virtues are, in varying degrees, intertwined with honor.

There was a degree to which cowboys didn't care what others thought. When they were looked down upon because of the nature of their work on the frontier range, they didn't care. In matters of honor—courage, skills, toughness, endurance, work ethic, and honesty—however, they cared very much what was thought of them and how they measured up to the high standards of their unspoken code. These attributes have been well-documented in cowboy history, tradition, and lore, yet among cowboys they were neither discussed nor praised. Rather, they were

expected. A cowboy who failed to exhibit them would not hold a job for long. A cowboy's severe violation of the code of honor, such as mistreating or harming a woman, could result in the loss of his job and difficulty gaining employment—even with an outfit a thousand miles away. Surprisingly, even in the days of the saddle, word of honor violation traveled quickly. If the transgression was serious enough, finding work would be the least of the man's problems. It could mean the end of the trail this side of the Rivers Jordan and Styx.

The cowboys' machismo, daring nature, and rawhide toughness are celebrated in film and literature, yet their conservative use of words and their dignified deportment were as much a part of their honor as those showcased attributes.

John Horton Slaughter was one of the toughest cowboys and fighting men to ever saddle up. As cowboys go, he was also one of the most successful, eventually owning and running a large ranch in southeast Arizona and serving as Cochise County Sheriff from 1887 to 1890, a time when the bordering region of Sonora, Mexico, had become the last sanctuary to the most notorious bands of outlaws and rustlers in North America. When Slaughter finished his short occupation of the office and returned to his ranch, the reign of the outlaw bands had ended, much of it at the business ends of Slaughter's pearl-handled .44 and double-barrel shotgun.

In his book *Cow People,* J. Frank Dobie shares a tale of Slaughter that demonstrates the unique humility even a successful cowboy possessed. When Slaughter was leaving his ranch one day, he came upon a man who drew up and asked him the way to Slaughter's ranch. Slaughter merely turned and, with a few polite words, pointed the way. When the stranger arrived at ranch headquarters he announced to the first man he saw that he had come to see John Slaughter. The man shrugged and noted that the stranger must have passed him on the way in, as Slaughter had just ridden out on the same road.

Such an exchange may seem ill-mannered by modern sensibilities, yet to those who knew cowboys and ranchmen of the time it would have been both expected and considered to be good manners. John Slaughter undoubtedly knew the likelihood that the man had come to see him, yet being the soft-spoken, mild-mannered gentlemen that he was, his humility would not allow him to presume that he knew another man's business or that the presence of that man indicated a desire for his company.

The cowboys' humility was neither spoken of nor aspired to. It simply was. By the magnitude of Creation around them and the power of the elements, they understood their relative smallness and insignificance. They were men of honor and pride without presumption, of grit but not bombast, of humility without meekness or pretense.

I wish I could find words to express the trueness, the loyalty to their trust and to each other of the old trail hands....I wish I could convey in language the feelings of companionship we had for one another.

CHARLES GOODNIGHT

Lord, keep me safe on this trail I ride, and if sometimes I drift from Your plan,

Guide me back gently to the land that I love, with the touch of Your awesome big hand.

The stars up above, I know You named every one, and I see my name written there.

One day I'll ride home, peace and joy for my own, with not one single worry or care.

"COWBOY'S PRAYER" EXCERPT

I hope I shall always possess firmness and virtue enough to maintain what I consider the most enviable of all titles, the character of an "Honest Man."

GEORGE WASHINGTON

I would be true, for there are those who trust me;
I would be pure, for there are those that care.
I would be strong, for there is much to suffer,
I would be brave, for there is much to dare.
I would be friend to all—the foe, the friendless;
I would be giving, and forget the gift.
I would be humble, for I know my weakness;
I would look up—and laugh—and love—and lift.

HOWARD ARNOLD WALTER, "MY CREED"

IN TRUTH, HE WAS A NOBLE STEED.

—Lord Byron

We ought to do good to others as simply and
naturally as a horse runs, or a bee makes honey,
or a vine bears grapes season after season without
thinking of the grapes it has borne.

MARCUS AURELIUS

THERE IS STRENGTH IN REFLECTION

When I first knew him he carried a Bible and a six-shooter.
He was gentle with horses, children;
his courage was never questioned…
When we got up in the morning he'd be sitting there by the fire,
as alone as the morning star, drinking coffee.

ROSS SANTEE ON HORSE-WRANGLER MARTIN DODSON,
IN J. FRANK DOBIE, *Cow People*

Two kinds of strength join together to define a person: physical and spiritual. Of the two, physical strength usually gets much more attention. With our cultural emphasis on physical fitness and outward appearances, along with the tremendous resources available to us in a country of plenty, we see many superb physical specimens.

Spiritual strength, conversely, is far less cultivated. Such strength refers not only to one's faith but also one's state of mind, heart, and spirit. It is this strength that enables a person to go on boldly and even cheerfully when the odds are not favorable, food and resources are scarce, fear rises, fatigue takes hold, loneliness pervades, and all seems lost.

Throughout history, the physical strength of cowboys has been featured in stories, paintings, and folk tales. They were never the bulky muscle types.

Instead they were strong like rawhide—lean, sinewy, and hard—possessing strength more impressive in a comparative pound-for-pound measurement. If they weren't physically strong they couldn't endure the rigors of long hours in the saddle, the harsh conditions, and tussles with longhorn cattle.

But what some might not realize is that many cowboys had spiritual strength that equaled their physical might. Spiritual qualities are largely intangible, and no true cowboy would say anything to draw attention to them. He said little about anything to anyone except to his companions. Captain John G. Bourke made this observation after his time in Arizona: "Strongest recollection of all that I have of border persons is the quietness of their manner and the low tone in which they usually spoke to their neighbors. They were quiet in dress, in speech, and in conduct."

Spiritual strength has no need to boast, brag, or explain. It endures, reflects, and then stands. It endures because it fills a vacuum left by the God who set eternity in the hearts of men (Ecclesiastes 3:11). Yet only an honest man genuinely reflects, for true reflection is inherently honest. Taking stock, he asks the ultimate questions: Who am I? Why am I here? What have I done? What have I not done? Where do I stand before God and man? Only when these questions are considered and answered in the silent recesses of the heart does spiritual strength surpass that which endures day-to-day and becomes that which stands forever and eternal.

IN QUIETNESS AND IN TRUST SHALL BE YOUR STRENGTH.

—The Book of Isaiah—

The history of every country begins in the heart of a man or a woman.

WILLA CATHER

How can we expect a harvest of thought who have not had a seed-time of character?

HENRY DAVID THOREAU

He is the word that speaks to us in the silences of the hills, and on the plains, and by the rivers. To listen is to be refreshed—is strength and peace.

THE OUTLOOK, AUGUST 17. 1901

It was a land of vast silent spaces, of lonely rivers, and of plains where the wild game stared at the passing horseman. It was a land of...long-horned cattle, and of reckless riders who unmoved looked in the eyes of life or of death.

THEODORE ROOSEVELT

THERE IS MOREOVER SOMETHING MAGNIFICENT, A KIND OF MAJESTY IN HIS WHOLE FRAME, WHICH EXALTS HIS RIDER WITH PRIDE AS HE OUTSTRIPS THE WIND IN HIS COURSE.

PAULUS JOVIUS

Earth has not anything to show more fair:
Dull would he be of soul who could pass by
A sight so touching in its majesty.

WILLIAM WORDSWORTH

Dear Lord God in heaven,

from my bedroll on the ground—
I can't help but see Your majesty in the stars
sparkling all around.

Your Good Book says You have a name for
every star I see above,
I know You're looking at me too, for I can feel
Your love.

"COWBOY'S PRAYER" EXCERPT

My heart is awed within me when I think
Of the great miracle that still goes on,
In silence, round me—the perpetual work
Of thy creation, finished, yet renewed
Forever. Written on thy works I read
The lesson of thy own eternity.

WILLIAM CULLEN BRYANT

LIFE IN THE SADDLE: PLAY AND LEISURE

What delight to back the flying steed that challenges the wind for speed!
Whose soul is in his task, turns labour into sport!

James Sheridan Knowles

Many cowboys were young men who were playful, good-humored, and competitive. Some of the games they played were very dangerous and demanded great skill. After all, what is rodeo but the grandest of all cowboy games, although roping grizzly bears and African lions (done by two cowboys who, bored in Texas, went to Africa to join with the British and fight Germans) runs a close second.

Even if you don't rope cattle or fight off rustlers for survival or entertainment, there are ways to bring the cowboy sense of play and recreation to your life today.

GET INTO THE SADDLE

To paraphrase Will Rogers, there's nothing quite like the outside of a horse for the inside of a man or woman. Arrange your next vacation at a guest ranch in the West or find a local stable that offers trail rides for cowboys of all skill levels.

HAVE A CHUCK WAGON NIGHT

Start up the grill and put on the steaks, season those pinto beans, and let the biscuits rise. Invite all your cowboy and cowgirl friends. Serve up the chow with your favorite cowboy music and wash it down with coffee strong enough to float a horseshoe. Arbuckle's coffee, still available today, was always a cowboy favorite.

HOST A WESTERN MOVIE NIGHT

This is a great activity to coordinate with a chuck wagon night. I think the old Roy Rogers and Gene Autry movies, now widely available on DVD, are much better for children to watch than most of the movies they are exposed to now. And Robert Duval, Kevin Costner, Tom Selleck, and Sam Elliot have kept the genre going with some wholesome, well-done Westerns.

SHOOT IT UP!

Cowboys loved their Colts and Winchesters and never took kindly to any attempt to take them away. Not much has changed. If hitting the firing range is your recreation choice, make sure all the folks—young and old—are thoroughly taught gun safety. Never compromise on this. Following three simple rules will ensure there are no accidents:

- ⊙ Treat every firearm as if it is loaded, even if you unloaded it yourself.
- ⊙ Never point a firearm at anything you don't intend to kill (boxes, paper targets, and cans are okay to kill).
- ⊙ Always check to see what is behind what you want to shoot at.

HOLD A COWBOY EASTER EGG HUNT ANYTIME

Scatter boiled eggs along a hill or large pile of earth. With two or more shooters and all safety measures in place, line up at the agreed upon distance and shoot 'em up! Take turns shooting and have a neutral party keep score. Eggs are fun to shoot because they explode when hit. Whoever hits the most doesn't have to buy his or her steak for dinner that night.

GO TO A RODEO

Gather up friends and family and spend a day, an afternoon, or an evening watching the events and taking in the sights, smells, and feel of horses and cattle, sweat and leather, good eats and old-fashioned fun.

LEARN TO TWO-STEP

A lot of community centers and organizations host country dancing nights. Look into what's available in your area or create your own dance night at home with some good country music and a two-step instruction guide or DVD.

PUT ON A HORSESHOE TOURNAMENT

Horseshoes is a simple, fun game that goes great with barbecues and can be set up in almost any yard or park. Check out your library or go online for equipment needed, rules, and suggestions. You might even find used equipment at second-hand stores or used sports equipment outlets.

EXPLORE THE COWBOY WORLD

There are some wonderful choices if you want to discover more about the West and cowboys. Explore the exhibits at the National Cowboy and Western Heritage Museum in Oklahoma City, the Roy Rogers and Dale Evans Museum in Branson, Missouri, and the Autry National Center of the American West in Los Angeles.

For a unique experience, attend a cowboy poetry gathering. Many are held each year all over the country.

PRACTICE THE ART OF COWBOYING

Get involved in any way you can with a children's home or hospital or an assisted-living facility for the elderly. Ain't nothing more cowboy than looking out for children and older folks.

FOR EVERYTHING THERE IS A SEASON... A TIME TO WEEP AND A TIME TO LAUGH. A TIME TO MOURN AND A TIME TO DANCE.

THE BOOK OF ECCLESIASTES

There on the tips of fresh flowers feedeth he;
How joyous his neigh...
There in the midst of sacred pollen hidden,
all hidden he;
How joyous his neigh.

NAVAJO SONG

A horse is worth more then riches.

SPANISH PROVERB

The horses paw and prance and neigh,
Fillies and colts like kittens play,
And dance and toss their rippled manes
Shining and soft as silken skeins.

OLIVER WENDELL HOLMES

WHOEVER IS THIRSTY,
LET HIM COME; AND
WHOEVER WISHES, LET
HIM TAKE THE FREE GIFT
OF THE WATER OF LIFE.
THE BOOK OF REVELATION

ROUGH TRAILS
ARE GREAT TEACHERS

Courage is being scared to death—
but saddling up anyway.

JOHN WAYNE

Tough times and trials are not the parts of life any of us look forward to experiencing. Indeed, some are difficult to discuss even in retrospect. Yet in every life some rain must fall. The deaths of loved ones and friends, sickness, the loss of a job or business, war, struggles with faith, and family conflicts are but a few of the trials that impact our lives. What determines the character of a person is not how many or what kinds of storms fall upon him but how he rides through the ones that do.

General George S. Patton Jr., one of the most renowned U.S. cavalrymen to sit in the saddle, once noted that success was not defined by being on top. "In our great country, most any fool can be a success at something...Success is how high you can bounce when you hit bottom."

Cowboys faced the same struggles and trials we do—and then some. Their work exposed them to danger, serious injury, and death far more frequently than most people today experience. Cowboys could be rolled on by a fallen horse, killed by rustlers, trampled by a stampede, bitten by a rattler, struck by lightning,

or die from hypothermia. And that's just a few of the potential fates!

Death and danger were constant companions, yet cowboys saddled up and rode without complaint or self-pity. It is this spirit combined with courage that prompted Charles Goodnight to observe, "Cowards never lasted long enough to become real cowboys." Those cowboys who saw the most rough trails, tough country, hostile Indians, bad men, rogue cattle, and hard times were the men with the most knowledge, wisdom, and generally the strongest character. When a young cowboy had questions, he wouldn't go to an inexperienced cowpoke. No, he would go to the man who had ridden through the storms because those who persevere see and understand things that those with easier paths cannot.

Do I wish then for more trials to increase my wisdom and understanding? No. I would rather make a deal. No more "understanding sought" in exchange for "no more trials given." The good Lord would likely shake His head and say, "My thoughts are not your thoughts, nor are your ways My ways."

That I cannot understand Him or the reasons for trials and suffering ultimately matters not. I rest in the faith that He has gone to prepare a place for me in the "sweet by and by." My home lies not on the blue prairie or high desert but across Jordan on an endless range beneath a cloudless sky. There, with Him, waits my only home. This sojourn we call life is just a long ride for His brand through hostile country.

Against the timeline of man's past and the eternity beyond, a life of a hundred days is little different than one of a hundred years. It matters not what I ride through but how I ride through it. It matters not what others think so long as when I cross the last river and ride up heaven's bank, my Jesus will say to me, "You were faithful to the brand and rode with grit and sand."

COURAGE CAN ACHIEVE EVERYTHING.

Sam Houston

The brave man is not he who feels no fear,
but rather is the man who subdues fear and
bravely encounters danger.

LORENZO DE ZAVALA

NO HOUR OF LIFE IS WASTED THAT IS SPENT IN THE SADDLE.

Winston Churchill

In God's wildness lies the hope of the
world—the great fresh unblighted,
unredeemed wilderness. The galling harness
of civilization drops off, and wounds heal ere
we are aware.

JOHN MUIR

I shall never surrender or retreat.

WILLIAM B. TRAVIS, AT THE ALAMO

Wherever man has left his footprint in the
long ascent from barbarism to civilization,
we will find the hoofprint of a horse beside it.

JOHN TROTWOOD MOORE

WHEN WORDS ARE
MANY, SIN IS NOT
ABSENT, BUT HE
WHO HOLDS HIS
TONGUE IS WISE.

THE BOOK OF PROVERBS

SILENCE OFFERS WISDOM

The trail is the thing, not the end of the trail.
Travel too fast and you miss all you are traveling for.

Wisdom, understanding, and discretion are three virtues linked to, yet separate and distinct from, knowledge. One may have vast intellectual knowledge but no wisdom. Conversely, one may have great wisdom without any formal education. The acquisition of these three great virtues requires an openness of mind and heart and the kind of distraction-free environment which, in our times, must be self-imposed.

Cowboys never readily accepted "knowledge," "facts," or "truth" just because people of power and influence extolled them. In the true spirit of the American West, they preferred to do their own thinking and reasoning. A prime example? In northern New Mexico in 1886 there was an effort to form a union of small cattlemen and cowboys. The enterprise was doomed from the start. Aside from a few other factors, the cowboys' independence of thought, deportment, and action ensured that the movement would never succeed. A group or sheep mentality didn't suit them. And it never would.

The stillness and silence in which they lived and worked allowed for the development of their minds and the cultivation of thought to the same degree that both areas of growth have been trampled by our race for success, goals, and possessions. Cowboys would not merely repeat what professors said or what they heard in the media, movies, or latest songs and call it "fact." They had to think through important decisions and issues for themselves; fortunately, they had an unobstructed environment in which to do so. The result? Men of the range were not easily impressed, swayed, manipulated, or led.

Some of the most profound and practical wisdom I've heard has come from cowboys and ranchers. It is the rigors of this life along the solitary trail that infused cowboys with the wit and wisdom now legendary in their poetry, song, and lore.

GO WEST, YOUNG MAN, AND GROW UP WITH THE COUNTRY.

Horace Greeley

But who can paint like Nature? Can imagination boast, amid its gay creation, hues like hers?

JAMES THOMSON

As if for the first time, indeed, creation noiselessly sank into and through me its placid and untellable lesson, beyond—O, so infinitely beyond!—anything from art, books, sermons, or from science, old or new. The spirit's hour—religion's hour—the visible suggestion of God in space and time—now once definitely indicated, if never again.

WALT WHITMAN

Cowboys call no man master.

THEODORE ROOSEVELT

Be still, and know that I am God.

BOOK OF PSALMS

FOR THE WONDERFUL BRAIN OF MAN HOWEVER MIGHTY ITS FORCE HAD NEVER ACHIEVED ITS LORDLY PLAN WITHOUT THE AID OF A HORSE.

Ella Wheeler Wilcox

Never ask a man about his past.

COWBOY WISDOM

A closed mouth gathers no boots.

COWBOY WISDOM

FAITH IS THE BEST COMPANION FOR THE JOURNEY

*Cowboys at the turn of the century had a very special feeling
about God and still do. They understood the vastness
of nature and the elements which they faced daily,
and the importance of spending time alone in
the presence of the Almighty.*

JACK TERRY, *Prayers Along the Trail*

Faith tended to come naturally for cowboys. That faith was simple but strong. Cowboys knew little of theology and didn't care much about it. Their education was that of experience—as riding men, travelers, and sometimes wanderers. In the creaking leather seat of their studies, they covered more miles and observed more than those whose education took place in small, roofed, claustrophobic rooms. They watched the sun and moon move across the sky, saw the seasons change, noted the movements of stars around the Milky Way's creamy swath, and were well aware of the one star that never moved when they pointed a herd north toward Abilene, Ellsworth, or Dodge.

They saw how wild critters innately knew how to take care of themselves—what to eat, what to avoid, and how to find shelter from storms and enemies. Mothers instinctively cared for and protected their young. Mountain lions knew how to blend with the landscape, seeing while not being seen. Bighorn sheep took to rocky slopes and ledges as easily as ducks to water.

Cowboys saw righteousness and wickedness, good men and bad ones, times of plenty and of struggle. They rode on pleasant days but also through terrible storms when stopping was not an option. Burning in the summer, freezing in the winter, riding through rain and snow, feeling the power of a hurricane as it battered and flooded the coastal plains or watching a tornado rip up range and trees, they saw and felt the brunt of nature's power.

In it all, for men who observed more than they talked, there was much to learn and understand. Equally clear was that much could not be known or understood. Unlike many educated men, cowboys had no problem acknowledging both.

Faith is difficult to define. The apostle Paul, in a succinct fashion pleasing to any cowboy, took a good stab at it: "Now faith is the assurance of things hoped for, the conviction of things not seen" (Hebrews 11:1).

Cowboys saw enough on the Western range, from deserts below sea level to snow-capped peaks above the timberline, to know that there was One greater than them and greater than all that lived, grew, and existed around them. This quiet conviction of things unseen, and thus unknown, gave way to calm assurance of things hoped for along the sojourn and at the trail's end.

All want to know the unknown. Cowboys were no exception, but they knew how to be content with what they did know. To ride hard for the brand, shoot straight, speak the truth, and do right according to their understanding was enough. For the rest, for what was beyond their control, they let the chips fall where they would. Theirs was a simple faith: If they honored what was known within and that made manifest beyond, a righteous God who knew and saw all things could be trusted to settle the rest.

Any one thing in the creation is sufficient to demonstrate a Providence to an humble and grateful mind.

EPICTETUS

Now faith is the assurance of things hoped for, the conviction of things not seen.

HEBREWS 11:1

GOD TOOK A HANDFUL OF SOUTHERLY WIND, BLEW HIS BREATH UPON IT, AND CREATED THE HORSE.

Bedouin Legend

IT IS HEAVEN UPON EARTH TO HAVE A MAN'S MIND MOVE IN CHARITY, REST IN PROVIDENCE, AND TURN UPON THE POLES OF TRUTH.

Francis Bacon

Heaven is not reached at a single bound;
But we build the ladder by which we rise
From the lowly earth to the vaulted skies,
And we mount to its summit round by round.

JOSIAH GILBERT HOLLAND

May He support us all the day long, till the
shades lengthen, and the evening comes,
and the busy world is hushed, and the fever
of life is over, and our work is done! Then
in His mercy may He give us a safe lodging,
and a holy rest, and peace at the last.

JOHN HENRY NEWMAN

IS IT SO SMALL A THING
TO HAVE ENJOYED THE SUN,
TO HAVE LIVED LIGHT IN THE SPRING,
TO HAVE LOVED, TO HAVE THOUGHT, TO HAVE DONE?
MATTHEW ARNOLD

PATIENCE GETS THE JOB DONE

The only way to drive cattle fast is slowly.

COWBOY WISDOM

Our world is more hurried than ever before. On streets and highways, in stores, offices, and homes, it seems everyone is in a hurry. When results, rewards, and changes are wanted, they're demanded immediately. When we want a family member, friend, or associate to change, we want them to transform in the blink of an eye. Young people want the monetary success and possessions their parents have (or more), but don't want to wait as long as their parents did to accumulate such resources. Patience is a virtue seldom demonstrated in these postmodern times.

The determination to hurry, appear busy, and achieve rapid gain is ultimately futile because it goes against the tempo of the earth and all life upon it. It matters not that we can build incredibly fast jets and cars. We still can't harness such speed into our own bodies. As J. Frank Dobie observed in *Cow People*, regardless of what we do, the tempo of the earth remains that of growing grass, ripening corn, meandering streams, and drifting leaves.

Cowboys understood the tempo of cows just as they understood that of the growing grass and the

run of rivers. And because their work depended upon this tempo, cowboys accepted and exhibited extreme patience. Cattle needed to move slowly over the terrain so they could graze, drink, and rest as they travelled. Every trail boss understood how to make that happen.

This attitude and understanding was apparent in the melancholic songs, hymns, and spirituals cowboys sang to the cattle by night. "Bury Me Not on the Lone Prairie," "The Streets of Laredo," and "Lay Down Little Doggies" helped pass the time, and the slow, sad pace kept cattle calm at night throughout the long trail drives, lessening the likelihood of something startling them into a stampede. A cowboy riding at a gallop or run couldn't keep the tempo of the songs—they were timed for walking.

Dobie recounts stories of two Texas longhorns that found specific hymns particularly soothing during nights on the trail. One would rise up, stretch out his neck, and stand stone still every time one of the cowboys sang "Jesus, Lover of My Soul." A group of Confederate soldiers allowed another longhorn to live out his life because he rose and stood at attention every time the herders sang "Rock of Ages." And those Texas longhorns, despite their clear responses to the songs, were a much wilder and spirited breed than the cows around today.

The cowboys who had to wait for the slowest of the herd to make their way along the trail followed the Creator's natural pace. They were able to ride out the storms of life with the same patient endurance and determination they had when they rode the prairies.

NO BETTER WORD CAN BE SPOKEN OF A MAN THAN THAT HE IS CAREFUL WITH HIS HORSES.

Andy Adams

The course of Nature is the art of God.

EDWARD YOUNG

Character is a by-product; it is produced in the great manufacture of daily duty.

WOODROW WILSON

It is not enough for a man to learn how to ride; he must learn to fall.

MEXICAN PROVERB

ENDURANCE IS THE CROWNING QUALITY, AND PATIENCE ALL THE PASSION OF GREAT HEARTS.

James Russell Lowell

WE FIND IN LIFE EXACTLY WHAT WE PUT INTO IT.

RALPH WALDO EMERSON

PATIENCE IS THE BEST REMEDY FOR EVERY TROUBLE.

PLAUTUS

LIFE IN THE SADDLE: RAWHIDE AND PANSIES

Even the roughest, toughest, rowdiest, most rugged and most manly of us wear lei. We do it for the pure joy and pleasure of it, and you cannot tell me that we don't look handsome as men should!

AN OLD PANIOLO, QUOTED IN
RICHARD SLATTA, *Cowboys of the Americas*

No two items could seem more disparate than rawhide and pansies. Rawhide, sometimes called "Mexican iron" in early Texas, functioned as such for a time in both Texas and California when cattle and their hides were about the only things of value in both states. In addition to its use in lariats and saddles, rawhide was also used to make chairs, hats, chaps, bullwhips, playing cards, book covers, horseshoes, shields, bridles, nails, and anything else the fertile frontier imagination devised.

Rawhide offers extreme toughness, flexibility, and durability—all attributes that the delicate petals of the pansy can never match. Thus any pairing of the two might seem incongruous at best. Yet no combination could better symbolize the heart and spirit of the "paniolo," the Hawaiian cowboy.

In 1832, three California vaqueros, at the request of King Kamehameha III, arrived on the Big Island of Hawaii, and before the Alamo fell in San Antonio, they and their Hawaiian protégés, were roping wild longhorns on the slopes of Mauna Kea. The vaqueros taught the Hawaiians the skills in the saddle and those of the rawhide craft, including Spanish saddle-making and the design of the rawhide lariat. Paniolos soon altered the clothing and equipment to suit the climate and demands of the islands.

The Hawaiians took to the low-crowned broad-brimmed black hats, trousers buttoned at the sides, knee-high leather boots with low heels, colorful sashes, and bandannas. Soon they personalized the look with colorful, fragrant flower leis worn around the neck and as hatbands. Pansies and tropical flowers were among the favorites.

Paniolos were every bit as tough, skilled, and courageous as their Anglo and vaquero peers. Hawaiian author Armine von Tempski observed in her early life among the paniolos: "Every self-respecting paniolo rode—to translate an old Spanish saying—tied to death. To lose a lasso, or cast off from an animal once it had been roped, was a paniolo's ultimate disgrace, even though failure to do so might cost loss of limb or perhaps a life."

They hunted cattle on the rugged, dangerous mountain slopes and maneuvered the wild cows and bulls to the beach. The paniolo would then lasso a steer and drag the animal behind him out into the surf where both horse and steer swam to a waiting boat. The Hawaiian cowboy was one of the few breeds of cowboys that had to regularly contend with sharks.

Paniolos all were working cowboys, but in August of 1908 at Frontier Days in Cheyenne, Wyoming, they made history on rodeo's biggest stage. The handsome, dark, lean, and black-mustachioed Ikua Purdy, born on the Big Island's Parker Ranch in 1874, took first place, claiming the World's Steer Roping Championship. His paniolo companion, Archie Kaaua, took third place. The speed, grit, and skill of these island cowboys with flower leis on their black vaquero slouch hats took everyone, spectators and competitors alike, by surprise.

I doubt there is a culture of men who have embodied the virtues of strength, toughness, and courage fused with gentleness, humility, hospitality, and love toward family and friends better than the Hawaiians and Samoans of the South Pacific islands.

Paniolos, men as comfortable throwing a lariat as stringing fresh-cut flowers on a lei, embodied manhood as steeped in machismo and pride as it was void of arrogance and bluster. So holo holo, paniolo ("so get around, cowboy"), but never beyond the setting sun to be confined to history's annals.

NOTHING DOES MORE FOR THE INSIDE OF A MAN THAN THE OUTSIDE OF A HORSE.

Will Rogers

SEAS ROLL TO WAFT ME,
SUNS TO LIGHT ME RISE;
MY FOOTSTOOL EARTH,
MY CANOPY THE SKIES.

Alexander Pope

NOWHERE...DOES A MAN
FEEL MORE LONELY THAN
WHEN RIDING OVER THE
FAR-REACHING, SEEMINGLY
NEVER-ENDING PLAINS.

THEODORE ROOSEVELT

YOU'RE NEVER REALLY ALONE

See that, son? That's God's own handiwork.
Look around you. This is my church.

REX ALLEN, ACTOR, AKA "THE ARIZONA COWBOY"

Loneliness is more a state of heart and mind than the result of conditions or circumstances. The loneliest people I've known lived in the most densely populated cities. Conversely, while cowboys feel lonely at times, I have never known of one who would have said he was suffering from loneliness. And there are several reasons why this is so—reasons that might help all of us find more comfort in times of solitude.

First, cowboys have the companionship of the mind. Their minds are in full working order, not having been dulled by the barrage of distractions delivered via technology, nonstop communication with others, and 24/7 media messages. Modern cowboys, to be sure, use some of these technologies but are not inundated by them in the way that most people are. Furthermore, a cowboy is not so easily amused. If he can bust a bronc or knock down a deer at 500 yards with a Winchester, the fact that he can shoot aliens or bad guys on a computer screen may not excite him.

Second, cowboys like what they do. Most modern cowboys know they could make more money doing something else, but that doesn't interest them. They like the companionship of horses and a good dog. They like the wide-open spaces, the lone song of the wind through the pines and its rush between a horse's ears at a full run. They value the freedom and their way of life far more than money, security, or ease. The days of solitude are part of that hard-earned freedom.

Finally, cowboys have and always have had spiritual depth and strength. They were often men of faith and, thus, adept at handling the tough times and difficult moments of feeling alone in the world. They understood that the Creator of all that they saw and loved along the prairies, rugged terrain, and river's edge was also with them in good times and in bad.

Yet the fresh air of the evening sighs among the leaves; the birds, those voices of the flowers, repeat the evening prayer.

JEAN-BAPTISTE-CAMILLE COROT

There are friends and faces that may be forgotten, but there are horses that never will be.

ANDY ADAMS.
AUTHOR OF WESTERN FICTION

There is nothing that God hath established in a constant course of nature, and which therefore is done every day, but would seem a Miracle, and exercise our admiration, if it were done but once.

JOHN DONNE

I can't tell you how much I long for you to enter this wide-open, spacious life. We didn't fence you in. The smallness you feel comes from within you. Your lives aren't small, but you're living them in a small way. I'm speaking as plainly as I can and with great affection. Open up your lives. Live openly and expansively!

THE BOOK OF 2 CORINTHIANS

This is the meeting place where God has set his bounds. Here is enough, at last, for eye and thought, restful and satisfying and illimitable. Here rest is sweet, and the picture of it goes with us on our homeward way, more lasting in memory than the sunset on the meadows or the lingering light across the silent stream.

ISAAC OGDEN RANKIN

To my quick ear
the leaves conferred;
The bushes they were bells;
I could not f ind a privacy
From Nature's sentinels.

Emily Dickinson

A COWBOY'S LIFELINE IS COURAGE

Vaqueros admired their fellows who were long-suffering,
patient, uncomplaining, and persevering, just as
Anglo cowboys esteemed men who worked in bad weather
or with pain, went without food, and tracked down
stray animals at all costs.
Courage—riding into the midst of a milling herd, for example—
represented another vaquero virtue.
The vaquero and cowboy expected and valued these qualities.

DAVID DARY, *Cowboy Culture*

"A man wanting in courage would be as much out of place in a cow camp as a fish would be on dry land. Indeed the life he is daily compelled to lead calls for the existence of the highest degree of cool, calculating courage. As a natural consequence of this courage, he is not quarrelsome or a bully.

"As another necessary consequence to possessing true manly courage, the cowboy is as chivalrous as the famed knights of old. Rough he may be...but no set of men have loftier reverence for women and no set of men would risk more in the defense of their person or their honor."

That excerpt from the *Texas Live Stock Journal* of October 21, 1882, summarizes the matter well. For some, courage may be seen as a noble attribute for those who have it or as an innate virtue. For cowboys this was not so. Among them, courage was essential, a requisite virtue of every man in an outfit. Certain faults or shortcomings could be allowed a man, but lack of courage wasn't one of them. Displays of courage earned no praise or verbal admiration. Like other unwritten laws of the cowboy code, such was simply expected. So prevalent was courage among cowboys that it was conspicuous only when it was absent.

And situational courage wasn't sufficient. A cowboy was expected to demonstrate courage no matter what came across the horizon or in the middle of his path.

Whether the men had to ride into a milling herd, stop a stampede in the pitch-black of night, cross a fast-moving river, negotiate dangerous terrain, push through a blizzard, or fight border bandits to protect a herd, they were expected to do so with unbending courage and resolve. Even at play, as when roping a grizzly or tailing a bull, any hesitation or hint of faltering courage in a cowboy wouldn't sit well with his companions—and might signify that, one way or another, he would not be among them very much longer.

Was placing such a premium on courage the result of excessive machismo? While machismo, among vaquero and Anglo cowboys alike, undoubtedly played a part, it was by no means the primary factor. Cowardice by one cowboy in a dangerous situation could result in the loss of livestock and the death of other men. That's why such a hefty emphasis was placed on courage among ranchers, trail bosses, foremen, and cowboys.

And being practical folks, cowboys frankly saw no excuse for any able-bodied man to be without courage. To them a man's courage represented something more profound than simply fitness for the job. When a man rode unflinchingly at their side through any storm or across any rushing river, such courage was considered to be a reflection of his strong character. If this test was passed, they'd say that a man would "do to tie to" or do to "ride the river with." In layman's terms, if a man could be trusted through the worst of circumstances, then he could be counted upon as a dependable partner in other situations as well.

Cowboys didn't often engage in reckless behavior or take serious risks without reason. But they also understood that earthly death comes for all. They just didn't dwell on that fact. FOR THEM IT WASN'T THAT A MAN LIVED BUT HOW HE LIVED THAT MATTERED.

A MAN OF COURAGE IS ALSO FULL OF FAITH.

Cicero

WHAT A NEW FACE COURAGE PUTS ON EVERYTHING!

RALPH WALDO EMERSON

COURAGE IS RESISTANCE TO FEAR, MASTERY OF FEAR— NOT ABSENCE OF FEAR.

MARK TWAIN

I LIFT UP MY EYES TO THE HILLS— WHERE DOES MY HELP COME FROM? MY HELP COMES FROM THE LORD, THE MAKER OF HEAVEN AND EARTH.

The Book of Psalms